IF YOU SO DESIRE

IF YOU SO DESIRE

poems by
Joseph Gastiger

LOST HORSE PRESS
Sandpoint, Idaho

UNIVERSITY OF NEW MEXICO

ACKNOWLEDGMENTS

Two of the poems gathered in this volume have already appeared—under other names, and in different form—in the following collections:

Benchmark: Anthology of Contemporary Illinois Poetry: "Soup"

New Voices: Poetry and Fiction from Colorado State University: "Same Difference"

I have to thank Bonnie and Ric, John and Jana, Becky, Susan, and Jean for their advice and affection—delightful company, co-conspirators, and dearest friends.

Cover Art: Desire, acrylic on canvas by Skip Lawrence. View Skip Lawrence's paintings online at www.skiplawrence.com.

Author Photo: Jean Gastiger

Book & Cover Design: Christine Holbert.

FIRST EDITION

This and other LOST HORSE PRESS titles may be found online at www.losthorsepress.org.

LIBRARY OF CONGRESS CATALOGING-IN-PUBLICATION DATA

Gastiger, Joseph.
[Poems. Selections]
If you so desire : poems / by Joseph Gastiger. —First edition.
pages cm
I. Title.
PS3607.A7874A6 2014
811'.6—dc23

2014028888

for Jean and Michael

TABLE OF CONTENTS

Lucky I even had money for smokes but I never went hungry, neither did you, back in our janitor days, in our steel-toed-boot, empty-the-slop-in-the-alleyway dawns—right around when old downtown was deciding to close all the pawn shops and lure back the rich, drive out the junk shops where Mexican girls in mantillas bought baby shoes. Half of my forks and knives, dishes and coffee cups came from that graveyard of commerce, like yours; most got as far as Wyoming, I reckon, no worse than before. Crossing the bridge, we'd head for a cantina near shacks that had no running water or lights. Theirs was a deeper poverty whose language I never learned. But the last thing I want is someone to feel sorry; that was the richest I ever was—indebted to no one, all of the time in the world to be young. We used to joke about moving to Quonset huts north of the city toward Laramie, once we got jobs making box springs or lawn mower engines for good. Come home grease-stained, crack open beers, maybe throw horseshoes till it got dark: that was the plan once we met the right waitresses and settled down. Mile-long freight trains divided our late afternoons into us and them, now and forever; unfolding story, unchanging fact. Slipping across the river down dirt roads, let me morph into someone else, someone whose signature might have been blown away by the wind.

TELSTAR

Back in the day when they built all these houses, not everybody even had phones. There was a booth, though, out on Stewart Avenue. I'd go past it all the time. Hardly a soul ever dialed in daylight: wives were already ashamed to be poor—puffing on Kent cigarettes like young actresses feigning amnesia. Most were exiles from Brooklyn; now they swept carports in potato fields. Plucked Japanese beetles off dying rosebushes, tweezed their eyebrows. Nightfall was different—strangers in kerchiefs walked home alone when I should've been sleeping, sobbing in syllables from the other side of the moon.

THE APOTHEOSIS OF ASTRO BOY

for John Bradley

High above Tokyo, resting his elbows on pillows of air, the boy who won't ever grow older guards the whole world. He woke up from a car accident and could fly, coruscate heat rays from his eyes, fire torpedoes from his hydraulic arms. But father won't love the thing he's become— nine-year-old Tobio, killed in the crash, can't be replaced by a doll blasting bullets from his ass. Though he speaks sixty languages, Astro Boy can't even whimper "why?" So he's sold to a robot circus, does tricks. Ham Egg, the top-hatted ringleader, figures it's time a mechanical army got rid of us all. Only our atomic ghost is brave enough to save the earth now, soaring toward doomsday in his black underpants.

HARM'S WAY

What was I, five? six? Glad to walk envelopes down the block, to hear the mailbox clunk when I let go. I didn't notice that cream-colored DeSoto rolling at just my speed until a woman cooed, *oh little boy.* She was trilling for the man in sunglasses beside her, how he had gotten lost, so could I take them to the highway, *don't you like treats?* Only the way he grinned scared me like a loose dog, so no, I never climbed in the wrong car. Nor did I disappear like the boy outside Food Fair, where his mom went to buy a loaf of bread on Halloween. Nor was I ever found tossed on the road like the boy in the box, back when ladies still wore long white gloves to church. I wish you had been as blessed, dear one, taking that path into the woods no one was scared to walk ever before. I wish you were as lucky, lazy, homesick, shy, as other pretty girls, and perfectly safe. Crews searched for you in cornfields, chat rooms, truck stops, but your steps were lost in the rain. Until the hunters came. Even the hoboes cried. All the poor woodcutters dropped to their knees.

THE INDUSTRIAL AGE

Before all the plants died, my father worked on trucks for Hoffman Beverage, went out on road calls to Pelham to crawl under broken down vans. Maybe a ball joint had busted, maybe a clutch gave out. He'd set up flares and crawl under the cab—getting it wrong half of the time, swearing at bolts, stubbing out Camels, scared he'd be fired. We didn't know. Not until, finally, Hoffman went broke, went off the highway, right through a guardrail, in his new car. Anyway. I remember the soda pop tower just off the Garden State around Newark, there at the bottling plant where he took me once when he was happy, no idea why—maybe I asked. Thousands of bottles rattling along on these conveyer belts, pulleys and chains—filling with cherry, and cola, sarsaparilla, and ginger—swiveling past, caps getting stamped on with a pneumatic hiss. One by one, they got sorted into crates where the first other people I saw appeared, stacking the pallets a forklift would carry out to the docks. That's how I figured the world got made— hand grenades, cigarettes, bazookas, toys, jars of Noxzema for my older sister, canned lima beans. All rolling past—empty containers filling with everything there ever was, sealed with a hiss, carted away to the neighborhood groceries that haven't existed for years, almost as lost as Crusader Rabbit and poor Tinker Tom. Part of me, still, wanted to live and die wearing coveralls, drop out of school—smelling the salt marsh, sulphur, syrup, and grease. Part of me almost grieved it was already gone.

PLENTY

for Jeanne

If that's what it was: the fleeting sensation this once you have exactly what you want, no more, no less—apple, some cheese, a glass of Calvados—sitting outside by yourself for a change while a half dozen bats comb the lilac air overhead. Nightfall, almost. Maybe it's warmed me twice, three times before. Must have been seven or eight in the small yellow kitchen back home, Saturday, once; I'd just spent all the allowance I'd saved on a model of Frankenstein—covered the Formica table with newspaper—eager and grateful, clumsy besides—my older sister was carefully painting every single piece for me, even the whites of his sorrowful eyes, dipping that oh much-too-delicate brush in those little glass bottles of Testors enamel, with all the skill she'd perfected from several paint-by-number kits. Ginger ale, chips. I felt so full and tearful all at once, knowing the world wouldn't stay this way very long, whether I prayed or not.

This was the fall Petey Gunn's dad figured he'd teach us how to fight. He'd been a boxer in the Marines, he liked to crow. In the cellar, he'd lace our gloves, hollering *don't drop your hands* as we went flailing, bobbing and weaving while he got drunk. Just after supper, I'd walk a half-block up to Petey's house, dreaming it wouldn't be me crying upstairs. My father didn't ask where I was going; maybe my sister was drying the dishes; maybe my mother was already putting the baby to bed. No one said boo except Walter Cronkite in the living room, and Walter was almost as sorry to be there as the dog. Since it looked like we all might die just before Halloween; missiles embossed with a hammer and sickle were minutes away. Ninety miles from *Surfside 6,* Cubans in coveralls clambered up gantries, commissars glowered in secret control rooms deep underground. I was out on the stoop, shutting the door, when I saw plane lights overhead—maybe the last flight ever from Mitchel Field. Dr. Kildare was singing "Three Stars Will Shine Tonight" on the hi-fi across the street where Sherry Trautman slow danced alone at the end of the world.

I didn't ride the carousel, grabbing for a brass ring; I was too small, my horse too lame. Hurried right by the sky fighters, ignored the flying cups; Mite Mouse wouldn't make me throw up upside down. Caught my breath by the pint-sized band—clay dwarves in powdered wigs— tootling as organ pipes spun them around. Just beyond stretched the wild arcade, where, with a couple rolls of nickels, I was as rich as any fourth grader could be. First, I squinted at love testers; teenagers squealed and squeezed, hoping for *Hot Stuff* or *Naughty but Nice.* Next, inscrutable Zoltar whirred to life as I fed him coins, dropping a fortune into my palm while he glowed. Meantime, two rows of Skee-ball games spat streams of tickets that, eventually, might earn me a shoehorn or comb. I'd inscribe a new luck charm, too, stamping one letter at a time into a shiny disc I'd always lose. Old cowboy star photos, joke licenses in hokey slang, slipped out of machines from before I was born. Mostly, I played the mutoscopes, flickering peep show cards I had to stoop to see, turning a crank.

Used to call it *Frogtown,* my cousin swears, right where Route 3 hits 21, along the Passaic River, boggy and rank. You'd take a one-lane road under a railroad bridge into the cul-de-sac, if you were brave. Meaning you'd heard, third-hand, about the bungalows, ramshackle houses back there in the dark. That's where *albinos* lived—entire families—last of a hamlet of Jersey hillbillies, allergic to light. Weekend nights, carloads of drunks would come gawking, egging some windows, blasting their horns, peeling away as soon as a door opened or someone yelled back. Later, at school, hoods bragged they'd seen, under the overpass, ragged men, whiter than possums, with tiny red eyes rooting around in the shadows. *Bullshit,* I wanted to say—even did—but not very loud.

FOR PETE SEEGER

Up and down my block, Pete, no one sang *this land is your land*—not for bartenders, hardhats, and cops. Not for our tribe—though, yes, *why so worried, sisters why* tolled from St. Brigid's precisely at noon. Sad wives lined up for the giveaway groceries outside the union hall. *Yo soy un hombre sincero* chimed that one peddler sharpening knives. Lots of us clapped when Mike Quill rumbled on TV, *damn the judges in their black robes,* but nuns had already beaten into us that we couldn't dance. Mumble and squirm was the best we could do ourselves. Indicted, blacklisted, and *Daily News'*d, you'd be a fool to expect us to listen; you'd be a fool to come strumming a banjo this side of the tracks. Jesus, you were a *communist,* scout leaders warned. Someone *they* listened to—Bolshevik tailors and Rachels in kerchiefs on Queens Boulevard. Not till I turned thirteen would such a dulcimer occur to me, follow my drinking gourd that far from home. Turns out the Wednesday you played at the school gym, my dad paraded with his legionnaires, gung ho with a dozen Elks and some Moose for napalming Hanoi. That's how come guards whisked you in the back way. Smell their cheap whiskey by bonfire light? That's the night I learned old songs, even from one so mild, can be dangerous,

We learned the lingo in Roy Siegel's art class, *crosscut* and *zoom out* to *lap dissolve*, dance moves in some grand catoptric trapeze act we were beginning to see as real life. Twenty-four frames per second we kept falling in and out of focus or harm's way, or love—then we'd ditch school with these cheap little cameras trying to show why. So there's a movie of me in a thicket, dragging a mattress behind the old jail. So Tammy Sue wanders Roosevelt Field aimlessly, ever sixteen. So there are people we cut out of magazines sailing past Saturn—ostriches, apes, fleeing from Nixon across album covers and posters of stars. But our true *auteur* was Danny Diaz, who wouldn't say much; he worked two jobs. He got his license and cruised Hempstead Turnpike, never went home. Duct-taped a camera to the rearview mirror and sped toward the city past all that was ours, filming the ebb and flow of traffic, neon, and the clouds.

LOUP GAROU

He was hurrying home through that thin strip of woods by the parkway that warm spring night when somebody cried *Run,* or else maybe he did since he needed to, all at once—needed to tear through the bushes, the vines, and leap that chain link fence, faster than he'd ever flown, as if crystals were breaking in his own blood—or he'd explode if too much of that energy got caught inside. So he found himself running headlong toward whatever and up over old junked cars, trying to outrun this animal ecstasy if only he could. Meanwhile ineluctable changes came over everything he could see—whirr of a rabbit, as he bolted, parting the tall wet grass, shimmer of surrender in someone's eyes, alone under the bridge. There was blood in his hair and he'd lost both his shoes when he came to the ballfield behind his old school where he had never seen so many stars.

Honestly, before cell phones we followed rumor, notes passed in algebra, looks in the lunchroom that could've meant *maybe*, or *no way*, or *why not*. Friday nights caught us hunting for somewhere to go as rain swept the dead leaves into dams on the storm grates of every block you didn't appear on. If I lucked out, some door would open into a half-world of couples half-dancing, wanderers all. Candlelight lapping from dusty Mateus bottles made us look grown up. I'd drop my coat on the Indian bedspread, weave my way back to the kitchen where, likely, someone sat rolling a joint on the cover of *Blonde on Blonde*. So we had time. Salems and Sen Sen. Hatful of dollars, believable alibis. Guardian angels decided what records kissed where we hurt. Sooner or later, I thought, you'd come; that October you never did, so I slouched by the backstairs, short as I was, which did no good. Mostly, we ached and yearned, hunted and pecked, forlorn, hinting at depths we were trying out words for, all lowercase. Ashamed of curfew, choked with patchouli, we floated room to room until gravity gathered us into the orbit of brief, unforgettable songs. That's when the murmurs stopped, suddenly realizing what would be lost, some of us flailing at inconsolable air guitars. I didn't know I would carry mine such a long time.

THOSE OTHER LIVES

I

Where I grew up we couldn't tell one bush from another, much less birds. We screwed up plenty of kinds of flowers, berries, bugs—so dragonflies were *darning needles* skimming trails too bright for us; those fireflies were lightning bugs wiped off my sleeve. And honeysuckle meant *bee bushes*, since they'd sting you if you ran. *Street rainbows* spread where any hose splashed gasoline. Fridays, the rabbi passed my house, blessing *good Shabbat;* all the same, we called jeans *dungarees*, and *Iris* meant a girl.

But rhododendrons thrived in dumps, azaleas grubbed through tar and slag, forsythia claimed wet dead places behind stores. Was it so lucky, finding robins' eggs? I found some everyplace—under magnolias after school, next to a mailbox, near the grates. I'd find them even through November, mostly where I wasn't looking—shells blue as the veins along your wrists. Was I so ardent once, that humid dark so sexual, that rushing home, I'd almost smell such need?

2

When I was growing up the radio ignited useless, pure desire. Anywhere we drove, some riff kindled it. *Who do you love?*, Bo Diddley whanged, hoodoo and mojo-taunting night working us dumb around blind hairpin curves, chained roads. We tooled a back way to the beach, hopped fences, scrambling toward the surf. I cupped a seahorse once. *And when I see the sign that points one way,* there wasn't anyone to answer why we ached, though I'd have believed if only I'd known how to swim, fight, French kiss, dance, you wouldn't catch me wheedling, *oh Donna where can you be?*

Where I went wrong was in the army of us clowns paddled for whispering through air raid drills, plus crimes against geometry, and snapping gum in shop. Was swiping Camels from my dad's sock drawer, only Jesus saw me gawk through *Playboy* at a corner luncheonette.

3

I grew up in shadows cast by the marvelous, which didn't come true—the future we were sure to reach, *Tomorrow* like they promised us—prophetic dioramas at the first World's Fair we actually got to see. I mean monorails and airships, opals set in lush pagodas, New York City powered by radium proved safe. I mean pearls farmed in Atlantis, also meteors towed by magnets. Though the bus took us past *Astroland* at least three trips a week, I couldn't sneak by the turnstile; rich kids rode those rides. Trust me, they looked like holy temples—small, fake sandstone Chrysler Buildings, like the city hall in Laramie in fact. If I'm still talking about Jerusalem, why else?

Why else would Donna Welicky refuse to love me, pitch my ID bracelet off a Bayville bridge?

4

Paper lanterns light the lawn. The cleaning lady and those cooks who speak no English count up dimes under the onion domes of their Ukrainian shrine. Maybe I should've called before First a hushed room, then his clothes scattered on the floor: *Through my fault, through my most grievous fault.* I'm sorry but I don't forgive you. But I do.

VOLUNTEERS

We went barefoot that summer all over the city from Central Park Zoo down to the Litvak junk shops where it was so obvious we didn't belong, tea-sipping merchants shooed us away with eighty-year-old brooms. Seriously. Nickle bag hucksters and Levittown wannabes slouched in the doorways of smoky apartments reeking of wanderlust, cat piss, and jasmine. Deviously. Dangerously. Sirens were everywhere. And out of windows propped open with paint sticks poured the same anthems, all weekend long—the Airplane's so unattainable Grace ever egging us on. I mean, who were we, anyway? *Fire-eating people. Rising toys of the sun.* Better to die on your own dirty feet beside Bernadine Dohrn. I mean, why would you *graduate?* Better to hang on as long as you could, before splitting for Idaho because somebody swore it was real. Some lines stuck in my head when I didn't want them to—for instance, once when I got on the subway too high, and the one-handed, greasy-haired veteran sighed telepathically, *the constant ride on the casket is mine. All mine.* I caught him flashing me the secret sign of the Phantom of Truth. But the girl I was riding with, she fell asleep with her head on my shoulder, and that whole night I must have promised her, *Everything we say we are we are.*

When it hit, your eyes seared immediately—beige mist horneted deeper, each gasp—and you ran and you ran between rearing bronze horses, galloping generals; skirls of canisters piked right above so the stirrups were all you could see. You ran and you ran by fence rails of the embassies, hotels of glass—some fell wailing, colliding around you on giddying streets, and still you heard through the stampede—you dreamt this—the cop who had lunged for you blocks ago, gaining, swap of the rubbery snout of his mask, swoosh and the crack of his iron-tipped stick, and you ran with the dwindling pack, you ran and you ran till you crashed to your knees—just thank God some girl yanked you onto the curb, swabbed Vaseline on your face. And you clung to her coat, shuddered and sobbed and got sick in the doorway of some garage on the back alley of meat warehouses, doubled up, grunting and gobbling air. Way too often, I've bragged over beer of heroic resistance, linking arms at the bridge, baiting the cops, outmaneuvering the National Guard. Actually, the biggest ran over the others, and I wasn't so proud, whimpering like an animal, fumes of pepper gas churning up wheezing and seasickness even to talk of them now. The real thing was scrambling and crying, afraid to turn back for the people we'd lost. Though we sang on the buses there, on the buses home—convoys left the armories twice a day, and what hopeless cause lacks for lovely songs?

We nix funeral flowers and buy panty hose for the organ pipes, to keep out the beetles so damned determined to clog any hymns. When I lifted the lid, I saw a steep cliff. The wind blew a gust of dry leaves in my face. Honey, the smallness of the world departs at night. My mother—restless, nervous, and generous, wanting, unsatisfied, and much martyred, angry befuddled at her own dying, not knowing what it was for but sourly sick of it, after her strokes and everything else— gasping, unable to see, and just about deaf. Which is how come our bodies ought to evaporate as soon as we die, and all at once become song, like every other in the world I cannot play.

UNDER THE REIGN OF CRONOS

for Sherman Raftenberg

That's what I named the Health Science Center—a grim colossus
beyond the trees, halfway completed, riding its pillars of rotted iron.
Stony Brook was a morass of God-awful buildings; the Lecture Center
(where I had psych, history, econ, and everything else) looked like a
gigantic upside down egg carton: pure East Berlin. Mud and cement
slithered and sloshed in the wake of those end loaders, wattling the
windows and plywood the color of shit. Steam vents and manholes
rimmed those paths, which is why your name reappears, all these years
after I left Long Island for good. They said you jumped (bullshit—
you tripped) clowning around coming home from the bars; somebody
dared you to leap through the fog pouring out of a pit. You were the
hippie who fell down a hole into the underworld—where vapor roiling
from ceramic pipe hits eight hundred degrees. The next morning, the
megaphones told us to strike. Crews put up fences, sawhorses, signs.
Midterms were scrapped; nobody even had to fake bomb threats for a
change. Kids from your dorm overturned cars. Those you'd expect to
spouted poems. Our bridge to nowhere dangled the dummies of riot
police. And I quit school. Much later on, I heard the law suits were
finally squared: the state paid eighteen thousand dollars—oh, plus a
plaque. A thousand each, they ruled, for every second you howled to
die, citing the proper clause, under the reign of Cronos, the god who'd
swallowed children, just to be safe.

ESKIMO IOWA

for Kimiko

One time, elated when some class was cancelled, we went exploring upstairs at McBride Hall—dawdled at cases of stuffed owls, coyotes, fooling around. We had it all to ourselves. It was April. Ostrich and wombat looked glad we had come. Poor hapless dodo waddled with us through its creaky museum. And we played hide-and-seek among dark dioramas, ducked behind antelope frozen mid-prance. Long before I clung to you in the Arctic, they'd locked the doors. So we spent half the night on the floor with the muskoxen eyeing us, nuzzling the moss— three of them guarding their calves just in case we got any ideas. I told you every way I'd been let down; you said, *It's all right,* and gave me that look, and till the janitor found us near dawn, dear one, it was.

Who was he—Ray? Roy? Ron? Some beefy ex-Marine prowling the long, locker-lined halls, catching the same strays getting high in the john. When I was lean, untried, teaching them grocery lists, conjunctive adverbs, and the woes of Job. He didn't seem so bad—asked me to supper, once—a little place back of a Laundromat. I brought some beer that night. There was a girl—dark waif who barely made a sound—frying potatoes while we drank. She'd run away, he said, still had a lot to learn. I felt the air between us scrape. I saw the magazines piled beneath his bed. Busted TV set, streaming snow.

PRODIGAL SON

School's out. My lease is up. Tomorrow, I'll be flying home to any grubby job at all until it's so creepy to live in my old bedroom, I jump on a Greyhound bus. I'll light out for parts unknown. Tonight, I ramble through Black's Gaslight Village, high since happy hour, humming songs for girls I hardly know. Black's is this asylum of hipsters: would-be Rimbauds from Bemidji, Plaths from Platteville, lanky Sapphos from Sioux Falls. They've drifted here, into a bipolar republic of bar waitresses and art class models uneasy in clothes. Turns out they're big people in little magazines. Turns out I'm standing in the doorway of exactly where I need to be, just shy of twenty-two, your perfect dope. A carnival eddies and rolls from one apartment to the next all up and down this colony of us half drunk with lilacs. Though technically we aren't dancing, there's no kinder word for how I drift away from what I couldn't wait to find. The girl I think I love blows air kisses, erasing parts of me. Years and years later, I still see her carried off by rum and weed and John Lee Hooker, beneath Japanese lanterns.

Tell me you never once wished you could vanish from grade books and bad dreams and old times when you meant to do something heroic but chickened out. Surely, you meant to punch Stuey Bloom's lights out after he slept with your girl, freshman year; thing is, he knew how to fight and you didn't, and they all saw. Think of a long list of humiliations—laughter in locker rooms, sniggers in class; how you felt squatting there, locked in a closet, until your dad finally unlocked the door. Tell me you didn't ever wish you could vanish from collective memory—start a new life tending bar in Ottumwa, running a donut shop in St. Cloud. Don't you think we have all got a right to be stupid once, ashamed, belittled, frightened and weak, without the ghost of it dogging us to every damned baby shower and beer hall dance? Go ahead, rip my face out of the yearbook. Erase my files, too. Why can't I be anybody I want for the likes of you—a submarine captain? A Corsican novelist nobody's read. Somebody you bummed a smoke from in June, 1974.

SOUP

Twelve below, more snow gusts over our whited-out road, plow trucks go riding back. Crows hang hidden in pines. Log smoke flavors the cold. My car tickers in a coma under its load of ice: nobody's getting through. The engine clamps dead each try; neighbors won't walk to town. I shave carrots we'd pitch, chop wilted celery, onion bruised moist in its outer rows. Peel a potato, lop off the spots; boil a picked bone into a stock. Throw in barley and hope for rich soup while I jumble out herb jars, basil, oregano, marjoram, rosemary—chosen by odor and sound. I invoke labels with little songs. I invoke instinct, dumb faith in the wonder of lentils, powers of garlic, vapor of golden fat skimmed from the pot like globules of banned medicine. One winter, Grandma showed me this story: three hungry soldiers limped to the village in snowfall, maybe deserters, only survivors of a Polish ambush; nobody asked. Peasants hid food under boards, in the barn straw, shrugged *look yourselves, we are bled poor*. I'm the officer nosing a cupboard for leftover peas. Fool bubbling stew from a cobblestone. I'm afraid still I don't hear it right, persistent stir of poetry ghosting hard miles through snow. Echoed messages beyond my ear, what men lost of themselves far ago in shacks toppled by wind. There is forgotten grain stored in burlap, blue corn for bread that could feed the wives dying at home because nothing is beautiful. Let me make what I can out of table scraps, water and salt. Add my common stone. There are moments when even I cry for joy I cannot contain, hovering over my sleepy wife. I shed tears on the vegetables, daydreaming my father's cough or the laughter of women who didn't love me anymore. Damaged love is the genius of soup, not the pepper or bone. It is longing become holy oil we pour into this page each time or this soup I so much want to give you. Taste my cloudy life in this bowl.

SKIN AND BONE

for James Wright

A couple of sparrows peck at suet on the snow crust. My groggy son clouds half the window from a blue chair, puffing out his syllable for birds that flit chimney to chimney, birds that stay behind this season, his birds. Last night, I dreamt of friends, in Colorado—me, Billy and John creaking that railroad trestle some ways north of town, clinking our train-smashed nickels still warm from the wheels. We'd tramped two hours to find the buffalo, grown hungry to hike back when there, below, the herd froze waiting, taken by sleep. Some gritty wind ruffled those shaggy humps, whirred flies round tails and haunches. We edged as close as barbwire let us. I could've leaned, patted the nearest bull— that close we crept, that whispery. I smelled the rancid cud, the dung yielding its heat. And as his eyes took life, so small, sheeny like jet sieved from a stream, the mildest look this world can bear asked, *What more than this? What else is there?* It's for that the ghost Arapaho dogged his track with reverence, not for the tongue and hide, the gristle gnawed for worry. There is a cure cast by the quickening eyes of animals. Once it has grazed you, so much rage—you'd think, I've dragged this with me, always, like a travois, my tree stump, some damned axe I can't use, wheel barrow of rock salt—drops from you, gravel trickling down a gully, and you step clean into an ochre range. The moon breaks kinder through crags of hogbacks creased by mule trails. The unprimed pump rumbles, kicks water sweet and cold. I stood that moment half the dreamer, half the dreamt in sight of buffalo, wind flagging to nothing across sage. In another life, I core this apple, eat my cornbread. In a lull after sweeping, before sorting laundry, I watch my boy craning to catch the birds, his eyes milk-drunk already, his hands batting the zigzag of their flight. What else is there to keep him company winter Sundays? What more than sparrows at the woodpile? They flicker, tap tap, startle and tick

still, alive, and no one's. I see my neighbor's arm throw scoop and scoop
of seed, pitting the snow.

They were all pretty drunk when the one called Bed Bug—at least when he wasn't around—figured they ought to go swipe all the fruit off the landlady's tree. Mostly since they were bored, and because Bug wanted Marcella to think he was wild, after she'd pulled away in disgust when his hand grazed her knee. So the four of them rumbled after the pears. Hell, if the widow hadn't been deaf, she would've whipped them until they bled, she always said. Though the fruit had no taste. Or, worse, it tasted like a bad idea, something you find out a little too late you never desired. But by then they had armloads of unwanted loot. Dawn's doves were all flitting about. Augustine said they should take what they could, to throw to the hogs. . . . Years later, he'd tell anybody who'd listen, someone had already paid for those pears: namely, the Jew God tortured for everything else. All because they'd talked back, thought impure thoughts, ran off with whatever, no matter why, Jesus was forced to wear his crown of thorns. All because a few boys could find nothing better to do on a sultry night, monks crept, one by one, toward huts in the desert, shaped like beehives. . . .

Little Jimmy tells half the truth. Look, I'm a lovesick fool who'd fall off a bus in Raleigh or Reno without any options. I would fill your apartment with pots of begonias, bluest I'd ever seen, paid for in Mayan jade from *cenotes* unknown. As if I'd killed men I didn't even know. Hell, I've dodged those crews in chains shoveling all day long, and some of them didn't cast any shadow at all. When you'd shine like the Chrysler Building at dawn, I'd be beside myself, skinning a rabbit in tall weeds way down by some rickety bridge. Mostly, I'd weep over cobwebs and corncribs. All through the airless night, we'd hear nothing but tow trucks and ambulances miles away. In my secret room underneath the yellow staircase, I might still hide—just in case—sugar and salt packages from the diners of my childhood. Jimmy mentioned you'd run away from a circus in Latvia into the nearly unbearable heat of the attic where we met. I can't sort it all out just yet. Not till my mission's done. Not before I can demolish the robots building those huge brass lungs serving the reptile gods of the radio empire. Yet I praise you with every not-quite-honest typeface of my own dumb luck. Wells of desire most hoboes can't find no more might open anywhere.

BATTLE OF THE SPIRITS

for Kathy King

In the old-timey mural back of the bar, above the menu for sausage and cheese, dreamy green hills roll around a medieval battlefield. Tankards of beer totter and reel, some with their helmets smashed; wine-bottle cannon across the cow pasture bombard them with corks. Stout steins assemble one final charge, time after time, blasts have knocked them all down, but look at their faces. These aren't soldiers; they're brewers and cooks. They're church people from Monroe, Wisconsin—hardware store helpers wielding those pikes, honest mechanics unfurling blue and white pennants, unfazed. Any moment, the limburger wagons and wheelbarrows loaded with raw onion will come, and so far no army of wine has ever beaten them back. Barley and hops would just as soon burn as give way to proud French grapes—at least in this tavern, middle of August, late afternoon.

Absently knotting his tie, the President feels a sharp twinge in the lobe of his right ear. *Like a wasp suddenly*, he could say, or the tip of a drunk's cigarette at some long ago dance. In committee rooms, clerks are adjusting the microphones, straightening the tablecloths, setting the pens in place. One of the secretaries tastes blood in the tea. Up a mountain, the first spray of gold leaves drifts off the top branches of aspen. Squid float ashore, mottled brown, across Delaware Bay. At the lunchroom where senators fret for the banks, a Peruvian cook brews a remedy good for his eyes. They itch and they burn. Children complain their tongues tingle. They're sent home from school. *It's because we grow too damn much wheat*, growls the traffic cop no one expected there. *Or the judgment of God*, chides the woman beside him in bed. Silverback apes refuse bread at the National Zoo. Already, capillaries have carried the holy contagion into the reservoir of the prophets, the cellular phones of the millionaires, and the chaste. By the rush hour, news crews have surrounded the President's catalfaque. Drone bees anoint his huge body, with honey and wax. Out her window, the breeze wakes up a girl who's lain hypnotized by her pre-calculus. A boy calls to an owl in the dead tree.

Lord of the crossroads, settler of scores, do this for me. When Merope took up with her cocky young soldier, I wanted to kill him, but he's twice my size, and distraught as I was, I'm no good with my fists. Pay him back twice as bad. Riddle that swaggering bastard with stinking sores. And if you pity me, generous Mercury, whisper Merope back to my bed, eager as she once was.

How could we tell what lay beyond, except go see? And so after the right prayers were intoned, the blood of many bulls splashed on the tiles, wine casks all emptied, after the rafts of flowers went by, we set sail and two moons waxed and waned before we came ashore, but even far out from land, we could smell the trees. Heaps of resin from young myrrh trees, cinnamon, ebony—these sweetened the air before we came near. Here the houses were set on poles, with sturdy ladders leading up them, beehive-shaped houses, the ochre hills shimmered behind them. Here we brought our papyri, tortoise shell combs, copperware, jugs of oil—goods we could trade for the ten thousand things we'd never seen. Here, in fact, we found figs and birds, ostrich plumes, ivory, drums of rhinoceros hide, tears of red glass. Here, they said, was a land rich in dwarves and giraffes. That was when Perehu came up to greet us with his Queen Eti riding an ass, she who was too heavy to take even a few steps. And he said to me, *Why have you come to this land your people do not know? We come hoping to find*, I said, *the home of the pygmy god Bes in the country where houses stand in the trees over the water, and one may sell green agates from the land of Amu.*

THE DEMONIAC'S WIFE

They came to Jesus and saw the demoniac sitting there,
clothed and in his right mind, the very man who had had the legion,
and they were afraid.

—Mark 5:15

Some holy man blows into town, this one a little more haggard than most, and by mid-afternoon, he's gathered a crowd. Mothers line up with limp children in tow, and what else can they do when he holds out his hands, mutters a few strange words? One baby coos; another's eyes flutter open to light. As if I'd never seen that trick before. As if I'd never seen desperation liquefy, solidify, into hope that will dull any pain, drag any weight, well, for a while, until it melts, and you're back where you were—hollow. Soon enough, some fool cries, *There goes that lunatic from the tombs*, and I'm frantic again, but there's no place to hide except among these shit-caked stones, out where hyenas split open bones of executed thieves. When I see my husband fall to his knees, even a long way off, part of me wants to believe he'll be cured, part of me wants to die right then and there because that's how it is once you've watched someone you love destroy all you had. Who'll run to welcome him back to whatever we haven't lost? Who'll chase my demons away when they come after me in the dark next time? Who'll take me in when I've got to go begging, when all the neighbors say, *Thanks to you, thanks to you, woman, the pigs all drowned.*

QUIVIRA

By the time I realized the Turk had been lying—there was no gold out there—it was too late to turn back empty-handed. That was the truth. We'd staggered much too long across the endless grass, left our lice and strange fever behind in too many towns. So the priest who was still alive asked us to kneel, held up a cross, muttered in Latin the loneliest phrases men ever formed. And he spoke about Jesus off in the desert, tempted for forty days, urged by the devil to transform ugly stones into bread. I'm not saying I listened, but that's when it came to me those who survived had to invent someplace to make our suffering and sorrow mean something more. What if there were a kingdom some of us saw, some of us even walked, where we were welcomed, fed, healed, and sent home? What if we weren't beggars now but emissaries of some enchanted place where even beggars were treated like lost angels rather than thieves? I didn't have to convince a single soldier who marched or crawled with me to Mexico, yes, we'd found Quivira—yes, it was just as stories say: a serene city with walls made of amber, and lissome women serving us roast meat on platters of gold.

He would have rotted away before winter, scraping at ever more furious sores, but when she promised a new list of traitors, he said, *Come in.* Stewed in the bath for a little while more, knotting a washcloth around his head, resting his elbows on the plank he used as a desk. The way she looked at him made him feel faint, smaller than he was. He'd been a doctor, summoned at night to the boudoirs of rueful roués. Marat was sure the soul swam in the fluid surrounding the brain. He'd written papers describing what sunlight could do to soap bubbles, lectured on gleets. Franklin kept sending letters on phlogiston, prisms, and chimes. Now as she slipped the long knife from her dress, he might have chided, *How unnecessary,* if she didn't shimmer like every tableau of the Virgin he'd dreamt. The toad prince of the *sans culottes,* sage of the sewers, felt more heartsick than afraid or surprised. In a summer of famine, Marat was already dying of bread.

Both sides tell the same story—they're all blown up or buried alive by the end of the war—but you get to decide whom we turn into monsters, whose story counts. Beyond the wire in watery craters, churned into whirlpools of rat-ridden muck, boys driven mad by the shelling couldn't help becoming something else. They'd appear after dark, shambling out of the fog, scrambling over a hill like a pack of wild dogs, going after the blinded, snatching tins from the dead. Anything to survive in a carrion world a few hundred yards wide but a thousand years long—oat fields crisscrossed by wagon tracks winding toward villages no one could find. The worst off became *ghouls*—so the old timers said—ragged, hollow-eyed grave robbers who'd run away. Most couldn't tell you what army they'd come from, not anymore. But that isn't the only version. Trust me. Files that next to nobody reads describe the renegades simply as men who'd decided *enough*. Tommies and *poilus*, doughboys and gerries, crawled out of trenches to join a mongrel nation, a beggar's commune, a tribe.

Body Electric

Besides those frantic, eponymous coils, frizzling through every mad scientist's rave, Tesla built gizmos like Pavlova danced—spark plugs and neon signs; fluorescent lamps, speedometers. All in his head, before he'd even buttered his toast. Neighbors watched him shoot lightning bolts from his bedroom, half a mile high. When he'd perform at fairs, crowing as megavolts leapt from his baton and writhed through the corn, onlookers gasped at the sorcerer, haloed in St. Elmo's fire.

Tesla and the Pigeons

Don't act surprised. Anybody who designs death rays in his sleep's bound to be scared of heiresses in pearls, and starlets in sarongs. Hide away in hotels, and take comfort in threes: three napkins, three cubes of sugar with tea. Three times, he'd circle a bench so each pigeon knew it was him. There he'd sit with his darlings in the moonlight, as they'd peck algorithms in birdseed, choreographing the vagaries of desire.

Tesla's Old Toys

Some November days, all I want to do is go rooting through junkyards collecting these artifacts—tone wheels and triodes, wounded arc converters—not that I'd ever know what to do with them. Or comprehend. Tone wheels, for one, *interrupt radio signals from antennae*—okay, so far—*heterodyne with them*—Greek to me—*to produce a shrill whistle*—easily heard, over some headphones what joe in his right mind would happen to buy?

Afterglow

Once Tesla died, the FBI stashed his papers no one knows where. That's why the world of Captain Nemo wasn't to be. Art deco airships floating past Paris, electric cars, run by thought waves—all his wonders sank in the harbor of half-baked ideas. Sometimes, they'd surface, though on the covers of pulp magazines—pictures for space romances I couldn't read. A falcon-headed Horus, say, rolling the dice in a Martian saloon, or a half-naked chanteuse, limp in some robot's arms.

LA GUERRA IGNORADA

You couldn't see them, but they'd be out there, waiting, crouching behind rocks, scattering nails along ivory roads that didn't go anywhere. News came of bandits in the dark who'd scrubbed verandas on their knees, nubile and sullen but for half-heard cries before dawn. Armed now with pikes and broken shears, hiding at night in the wadis and dunes, they cut our lines, poured sacks of arsenic in the wells. Under siege we ate sardines, we sang arias, smelled lemon thyme while admiring the moon. Under siege, we grew sentimental for *Carmen, turrón,* and ice. And, yes, flirted more ardently with a neighbor's cousin or wife. Oh, but legionnaires took off into the glare, sand, and *chumberas* in canvas shoes, taking our horses, hunting gazelles up in the hills. I remember their jackets, sour and stained, wearing an emblem as sorry as sad; a weary camel beside a palm tree nowhere to be found. Since our airplanes were antique, flags few half-mast in our little toy city of penny arcades. Daring pilots dropped tires filled with water, bursting when they hit the ground.

BROTHER LEADER ESCAPES

A word from my book can destroy the world, it can make the world explode!
A word from my book can redeem the world and change the value of things.
Their weight. Their volume. Everywhere and always!
Because I am the Gospel! I am the Gospel!

—Muammar Qaddafi

It wasn't him. He'd doubled back, drawn by the call to prayer, so when a Mirage swept over the motorcade, he wasn't there. Cameras lie. Besides—you can be so naive. The King of Kings gobbled fistfuls of garlic, a bowl of chicken broth, trying to think of the name of a girl he'd danced with at West Point. Who'd have believed back then, when he couldn't even cut leather for shoes, one day newspapers would proclaim his wisdom forty times per page? *I saw this guy running, I followed him,* pleaded the cook—except witnesses lie. Tacho didn't jump out of a smoldering Jeep. Because *I'd like Libya to be a black country. Libyan men all ought to marry black women; all Libyan women should marry black men.* I rest my case. That's what Il Duce blustered in Bucharest, patting his testicles— to be protected , he whispered to Clara, from the evil eye. There at the Condor Nightclub with his cronies, over and over he'd thank Carol Doda, signing her drainpipe, *Genius of the Carpathians.*

BROTHER LEADER EXPLAINS

What is the matter? What is going on? What do you want?

—Muammar Qaddafi

I did all this for love, cried His Excellency, and apartment blocks rose out of the sand—wavered in midair before they all crumbled, melted away. He remembered how happy he had been at first; driving a beat-up Volkswagen through town, buying his groceries; the simple pleasure of peeling an egg. But with power comes complicated obligations, trepidations, exotic taboos. He couldn't fly over water, for instance. Couldn't even climb more than thirty-five steps. Stuttered on TV, praising those pears made of plastic and apples of polystyrene. Sadly, he never did abolish Switzerland. At least he'd renamed the months of the year—Hannibal sounds so much better than August, wouldn't you agree? No one can keep track of every typewriter, every Ramon with a sack of grenades. Sooner or later, the Danube of Thought dangles over a gas station. *Why is the world upside down?*, he's demanding to know.

IN YOUR OWN WORDS

for Marc Liblin

The old man on the beach kept on trying to explain how waves recapitulate sine and cosine; beads of rain ripple the sand dunes in ways he insisted would forecast, if you could read, how smoke meanders, the ellipses of doves. He'd show you physics can create an island in a dream. And when you'd wake, get dressed for school, back on the other side of the earth, sometimes you didn't know whose story was real. Nobody did. Not a fat priest, dreading phonology; none of the sailors or hypnotists. Sometimes the songs you sang sounded like melodies from those caves. Yet you savored each word—*kare* for *water, rima* for *hand*—from faraway, lapping the shore of whatever it was you wanted to say. And so why would you call a shadow *une ombre*, when it was *ata*, where you belonged? Why would you ever betray your *varua*, trade for *esprit?* How many years would it take you to find the one woman who'd suck the same vowels in her sleep, someone who'd sigh at the moon as *ma'ina*, never as *lune?*

WORDS WE LOVE MORE THAN
THE THINGS THEMSELVES

Some tailspin in a turn of phrase stirs omens anyplace you walk. A cougar in the corn, or just a quail. When androgens of autumn and the halogens of light transmute even your poorest lies to song, ocarinas and kalimbas spill calypso through the opiate air. Say what you like: Those piers burned, and the birds were gulls. No bells gonged in the great beyond. No reason valences in sounds bring you to tears. I'll go on loving olives, no matter how salty, even if I never taste another.

If you were important, you would be somewhere else. All the important people have flown away, leaving their paperback romances folded on chaises longues by the pool. All of the dignitaries and starlets disappear moments before the explosions, gone with their cell phones and bracelets and spice colognes. If you were as blessed as they, you, too, would vanish—you, too, would wave down a taxi in Sante Fe, just as the jets release. You, too, would find yourself weeping to *Giselle,* as soon as tremors hit. If you can hear me now, you've been appointed no one to worry about—hiding in a cellar, coughing in a clinic, crouching in what, yesterday, could have been a laboratory, could have been a school. Long after this war ends, before the next one, someone in medals will lift up an urn of your ashes and howl for blood. He won't be your child, bitter, or crippled. Choices were made. You weren't counted.

What if I said one woman paints two hundred faces on a wooden door, each one the size of a half-lump of charcoal, or a sob? What if she paints just one face over and over, two hundred times? Wouldn't you say, *Please. Enough.* But it's the door to a house that caught fire, with people inside. Drive through a city one evening, late fall—Trenton or Camden, turning to rust—trying to find the last drugstore still open to your mother's pain. You don't belong, but there are plenty of doors you can't even budge. Someone makes circus beasts out of cracked vials and dull needles from the weeds behind Grant's Tomb.

BECAUSE SOME THINGS CANNOT BE SAID

Christmas and Easter can be subjects for poetry, but Good Friday,
like Auschwitz, cannot. The reality is so horrible it is not surprising
that people should have found it a stumbling block to faith.

—W. H. Auden

Perhaps on Good Friday the blue herons on North Brother Island pray
better than I do, or ever can; they'll wait for hours or maybe all day,
motionless almost except now and then, so very slowly with unearthly
patience one will unwind a crooked leg, or dip his bill into the algae
and oil of the East River for what it needs. Decades may pass before
any boat lands here, and so except for the lap of the tides, and for the
squawk and the scramble of stray birds, some of them so rare they're
practically gone, the heron preys in a veil of solemnity uncreased,
uncluttered by any word we know, which is what Trappist monks long
for, I guess—pure contemplation, sensation, surrender to rhythms we
hardly sense, interrupt, twist into typical dead end ideas, rather than let
ourselves gradually disappear into some holy gaze, like a man drained
of all thought after dialysis, while they wheel him back to his bed I have
seen people look up with such emptiness, you'd say they, too, have come
down off a cross. Somewhere past agony, beyond anxiety, full now of
nothing whatever to say—which I believe was how pale Lazarus looked
at his sisters, though he never asked, *Why did you call me back from wherever*
I was? This forsaken islet, with all its assemblage of relics and ruins—
desolate hospital, warren of leper shacks—here's where the Gerasene
demoniac danced his last tango with Typhoid Mary; here, too's the
circle of graves for those immigrants too sick to even totter ashore.
Here there's a morgue and a chapel so overgrown with poison ivy and
kudzu vine, almost no light finds its way into the corroded crypt of
Christ. There are Chernobyls in every city old enough to have to tell

its grandchildren lies about what happened before all the crippled folk floated away. Maybe they come back to us now as blue herons, which, if we happen to see them at all, seem to be standing as still as centurions—shadows of a no longer quite visible man nailed to a tree.

FABLE OF THE SHOES

for Yannis Ritsos

Tiny at first, almost too small to see, shoes sail the air, fall into culverts, litter the gulches and gullies of Texas—shoes made of ash, dander, and pollen, ice crystals, scabs. Shoes of the half-remembered, taken-away, never-returned. Oh, but what fine workmanship in the stitching, the lacing, the soles. A soft rain of shoes patters the roof of the morose ex-president. The senile general growls at the ceiling at night, *I can hear you. Enough, go away.* And weather forecasters say nothing except what we pay them to say. Once in a while, an actual shoe falls from a cubbyhole in the sky—shoe of an old friend, or a girl you walked home from school. Once in a while, you still may find one along a roadside outside the city: a small cry for justice, a disconsolate shoe.

PARABLE OF THE BLIND

for Ishmail Kadare

After his best general was slain, Basil II, Byzantine emperor, rounded up all of his prisoners of war—fifteen thousand, most stories say—roped them together in gangs of a hundred and burned out the eyes of ninety-nine—yes, they had tools for that sort of work—leaving one man half-blind to lead the rest home. In the heat of midsummer, they clambered up hills, tripped over stones, crashed into trees while one far ahead shouted warnings too late or too soon. Some began desperately moaning for water. Others tied rags around their seeping wounds. Weeks went by as they wove through woods blistered and broken, tormented by flies. When the Tsar of Bulgaria finally caught sight of them—how they'd survived, who knows—most say he dropped dead on the spot, horrified. Others say no, he lived three months, but never left his bedchamber again. Ever since, there've been tales about hunters straying too far into thickets after a deer, and finding someone covered in filth and rust crying *Please, which way is paradise?* Or sometimes, *Where have they all gone?*

FIRST PARABLE OF THE DEAF

for Marcel Schwob

What if we found a village where—and there are actually places like this, among the Bedouins, or in Bali—thanks to some rare genetic glitch, fear of outsiders, salts in the wells, people grow up unable to hear a sound. Oh, they have instruments, all made of rosewood and perfectly tuned; melodies transcribed in a script mimicking tracks that birds leave in the sand. Let's suppose they are lovely, yes, but no one alive's ever heard them; since they are holy, only the Ancient Ones are allowed. It is best not to hear the amorous laughter of *djinn* and *ifrits*, which, after all, is how most music starts out. By the same token, nothing so priceless may be thrown away; refusing such a gift is unpardonably wrong. And so there are ensembles and orchestras practicing, practicing day and night. And just now, as the last guest takes his seat, the performance begins.

SECOND PARABLE OF THE DEAF

for Maya Deren

What if we found a valley where—and there are still places like this,
deep in Belize and Suriname—Indians and Africans who slipped
through the swamps and got away live in that time before the first
ships came. Thanks to the jungle, though—dengue fever, and they're so
few—not many hear those bright birds before dawn. Some hardly hear
the capuchins high in the trees, but they know what ghosts say, stirring
the leaves just so. They sing the oldest stories in the world to their
children by firelight, all with their eyes and hands, night after night.
Yet that kinetic alphabet ever eludes even though it surrounds us. Their
language suggests nineteen different ways someone can turn and sigh,
each with its own blending of sorrows and delights.

ARLEQUIN ET PIERROT

after Derain

Get a look at them hotfooting out of that emptiness where town gives out and the desert begins, couple of jailbirds in old circus clothes—Arlequin stuffed in a patchwork of red, yellow, blue and green diamonds; floppy chapeau, puritan collar, unlucky undertaker's black shoes. Pierrot, of course, pirouettes in a clown's cloud-colored robe, tight little cap, Tudor ruff fished from God only knows where or why. Can't hear their song—Arlequin strumming his hand-me-down lute; Pierrot reluctantly fingering feathery chords on guitar: neither have strings. At Pierrot's foot, someone has left a jug , fiddle and bow, white tablecloth. Somebody's swag, somebody with no good reason to stay: carried away by a terrible thirst, or the local gendarmes. They stare bereft, as if they've been to see the children's graves, past treeless hills near the abandoned mercury mine. Yes, they've come back, guilty as charged of stealing the wren's eggs, strawberry pies, Columbine's heart for the ten thousandth time. Except she's gone, just before she promised she'd make her choice: insolent joker or moon-addled mime if she'd only decide. Loving them both, figures she'll never be either one's wife. Only their jealousy keeps her from fading back into forever, never again, in a small village somewhere in the Pyrenees long, long ago tootling a fife, out in the garden waiting for rain. Perhaps they play different songs, but they both tilt their heads the same way. Arlequin's tune trills empty boasts, mock-heroics, conceits. Pierrot's all pratfalls and bits of impossible longing mixed up with the folklore of birds. Always, he's wearing the face of a milkman man who's trailing his one true love; Arlequin can't wait to sell you a magic elixir or halfwit girl–she who got into his wagon convinced she'd find work as a maid. Fat chance of that. Pierrot's like smoke pouring out of a kiln. Arlequin dreams he is shoveling bones from the ovens for bread and soup. Inseparable they stumble toward one more gallows at dawn.

You could see it coming. One after another, the gumball factories all went to hell, and as soon as the last sardine cannery closed, I was out of a job. So I walked into places I'd passed by for years, curious what was left—no-name warehouses of candy and sea monkeys, pinwheels and useless salves. It's amazing what people can dig out of dumpsters behind decrepit dorms, the morning after hordes of unbaptized babies have to leave town: new beanbag chairs, hookahs and catalogs; gas mask I'd wear if I woke up and wanted to look like a bug. Of course, the bars were crazy. French legionnaires badgered a Buddhist monk, *Which one was better, Rootie Kazootie or Pinky Lee?* But the substitute teachers never complained; they took their assigned seats and worked on Sudoku. The last of the lotus-eaters wept as he boarded the train.

ALL THE TREASURES OF OPHIR

Two or three sacks of concrete at a time, he built a Jerusalem in his yard. First, the birdbath, then the windmill, a grotto half-hidden under the oaks. And if the signs were true, it was the smallest church in the world, or in Iowa—each wall a slurry of broken tea cups, Noxema jars, marbles and antique Aunt Jemima gimcrackery. All summer long, Crazy John went on encrusting his kingdom with mirrors, Christmas balls, old lady brooches and hairpins, Cracker Jax toys. Water gurgled in his pond, and daylight ricocheted off the blue geodes, garlands of scallop shells and cufflinks. I wish I could show you the mill's twirling paddles of Dutch wooden shoes; meanwhile, yes, dragonflies darted from window to window among the rhinestones and bottle caps—all of the gaudy treasures of Ophir spilled on his lawn. Wish I could coax you into that grotto where, in a display case, you'd find the head of deer with a red lightbulb for a nose. Flanking those photos of nieces and trophies were a pair of roosters—one of cracked shells, the other made out of old eyeglass lenses all painted black. Up on the altar, some mystery bone from a neighbor's dog healed old hurts. Pews of abalone frozen in Lucite, myrtlewood candlesticks. As you ducked out again into the garden, you'd hear *Twinkle, Twinkle, Little Star* chirping relentlessly from God knows where.

THE COLANDER

for Michael

The day after you graduate, after we pay for lunch, we pass the building you'll be moving into once summer ends. It's an old school, broken into apartments: three storeys up, three gabled windows, when the leaves fall. Nearby, we wander around in an empty mall for an awkward hour before we get on the road and drive three hours home. It wants to rain. Most of the shops don't open Sundays, some have gone bust, but here's a place that sells kitchen utensils, hot sauces, teas. What can we buy for you, part of me cries. How can I even try to explain how incurably sad they glow—teak cutting boards, chrome garlic presses. All we can buy. *Some day,* you say, *if I ever get paid*—black and white colander, way overpriced. Speckled enamel. I'm close to tears. Years ago, when I'd turn up in a town, I'd hit the Goodwill, Salvation Army—dicker for dishes, small tarnished treasures. Not anymore. But why would a thing like that make it so hard for me to say goodbye?

CORAL REEF

after Mike Nelson

Cripes, you're prowling a dream goons barge into by accident, knocked
through some creaky doors, into a warren of dim, ratty corridors,
decrepit offices, interrogation cells dotted with posters of the old
regime. Runaways hole up here, crash on the floor of defunct travel
agencies, before they stagger on back to the railroad yard, fucked up
on glue. That would explain the seats torn out of taxicabs, broken-
down fans rattling, busted security monitors flickering anyway. Other
rooms haunt you worse, almost. How can you unscramble these clues:
JFK wall rug art, a plastic tommy gun, that Halloween mask of a
clown? Any moment, the cops will nail you for trespassing, sauntering
where you don't belong, snooping around for a suitcase of anthrax,
or an old flame.

Riding the bus one time back to Fort Collins, I saw a flotilla of airships floating toward foothills that weren't there. None of it was, I mean, neither the ochre hills nor anybody waving from a gondola high above. It was as though a page from some atlas, long out of date, had just been superimposed on a clear blue sky. It was as though a contrary reality— switchbacks, those balloons—wanted to blot out the actual mountains west of town. Which was when I realized the life I'd counted on living, in that pure light, was something I'd only borrowed temporarily; it wasn't mine. Whatever lover or poet or drunk I turned into, it wouldn't be here, not after watching those ships drift away with so much I couldn't have. Sometimes, I dream I'm looking out a bus window at stubble fields, sagebrush and oil pumps along I-25. After all, that was where I used to ache to call home. If you'd told me I'd end up in jail in Georgia or preaching in Illinois, I wouldn't have known which was more likely, honestly. All I was sure of was, if and when I ever came back wounded and broke, most anyone I loved, owed, or longed to see again would've split long ago for some other town.

JUBILEE

A bright girl I see three days a week on the treadmill smiled hello today, never before. An old man at a gas pump grinned, singing doxologies without words. Wait, that was me. What November in memory swept away bedraggled asters and left me joy? Two, long ago. Both times, I'd fallen in love, and I said so. I was that brave. We walked through empty parks lit by chrysanthemums, listened for Angelus, kissed in the rain. Now, though, is different, stripped of desire's exquisite daze. More like exploring a city where strangers press palms together to sigh *Namaste*. The light in me recognizes her sister, embodied in you. As if whatever would follow us home so late belonged to something more real than the air, more real than any handful of phrases, lost in the abject corn. What if tonight we crept into the oldest church we could find and turned on the carillon—set the bells pealing, like after a wedding? Because, yes we can.

As if I were blessed enough to be one of those three robed men sharing a pipe out there in the shade of a peach tree. As if I'd been coaxed to write verses for oud and drum, verses you won't remember when we wake. The sweetest temptation the devil has is *Let me show you what's true.* You loved me in pencil; I loved you in India ink. The old men sit as still as stones. Maybe they are stones. Or maybe I ought to offer them tea and cakes. Sometimes the devil shows up in the marketplace, peddling his lovely scarves. I've never bought one, but after he's packed and gone, I wish I had.